HOW TO BUILD A PLANET

A little flying bug called ZOOMY lives at HQ and wants to join the fun.

See if you can spot her in every scene.

LADYBIRD BOOKS
UK | USA | Canada | Ireland | Australia
India | New Zealand | South Africa
Ladybird Books is part of the Penguin Random House group of companies whose addresses can be found at global.penguinrandomhouse.com.
www.penguin.co.uk www.puffin.co.uk www.ladybird.co.uk

First published 2025
001

Printed in the UAE

The authorized representative in the EEA is Penguin Random House Ireland, Morrison Chambers, 32 Nassau Street, Dublin D02 YH68

A CIP catalogue record for this book is available from the British Library

ISBN: 978-0-241-62326-8

All correspondence to:
Ladybird Books
Penguin Random House Children's, One Embassy Gardens
8 Viaduct Gardens, London SW11 7BW

WRITTEN BY MOIRA BUTTERFIELD

Imagine building a **new planet** any way you like and as quickly as you want. You could visit it for out-of-this-world holidays or even live on it with a starry new address – 1 Space Street. But **where** do you begin?

First, you will need a mega-fantastic team of helpers. A group of builders that can make **anything** and **everything** in the universe. A super squad that **might** sometimes lose a tool or spill a can of paint, but who will say, **"You want to build a planet? No problem!"**

But **who** could this **wonder-team** be . . . ?

BUILDERBOTS
HQ

MEET THE BUILDERBOTS!

SKIPPER is the boss. When the Builderbots are on a job, she's the one who makes sure it stays on track. And she's got lots of fascinating facts at her fingertips.

WHEELIE can drive anything, from a mega digger to a spaceship.

TOOLBOX T has a box that unfolds in a thousand amazing ways and carries every tool you can think of. He's got a thousand terrible jokes, too!

MUSCLES has four strength settings on his tummy: ***strong***, ***super strong***, ***mega strong*** and ***WHOA! NO WAY!***

MINIMO is the smallest Builderbot, and she's still learning her job. She likes to have fun, too. At the moment, she's teaching herself to juggle . . . Er, should you be using those hammers, Minimo? Minimo? *WATCH OUT!*

THE PLANET PLAN

TO-DO LIST

- Find a good spot in space to put the planet.
- Think about which other planets you might like as neighbours!
- Mix up the planet ingredients. (Earth has a great recipe we could use!)
- Start building! You'll need hills, mountains, valleys, volcanoes and more.
- Work out how to get the planet moving.
- Decide what the atmosphere is going to be like and prepare for the weather.

If you want a big building project to go smoothly, you need to start with a plan.

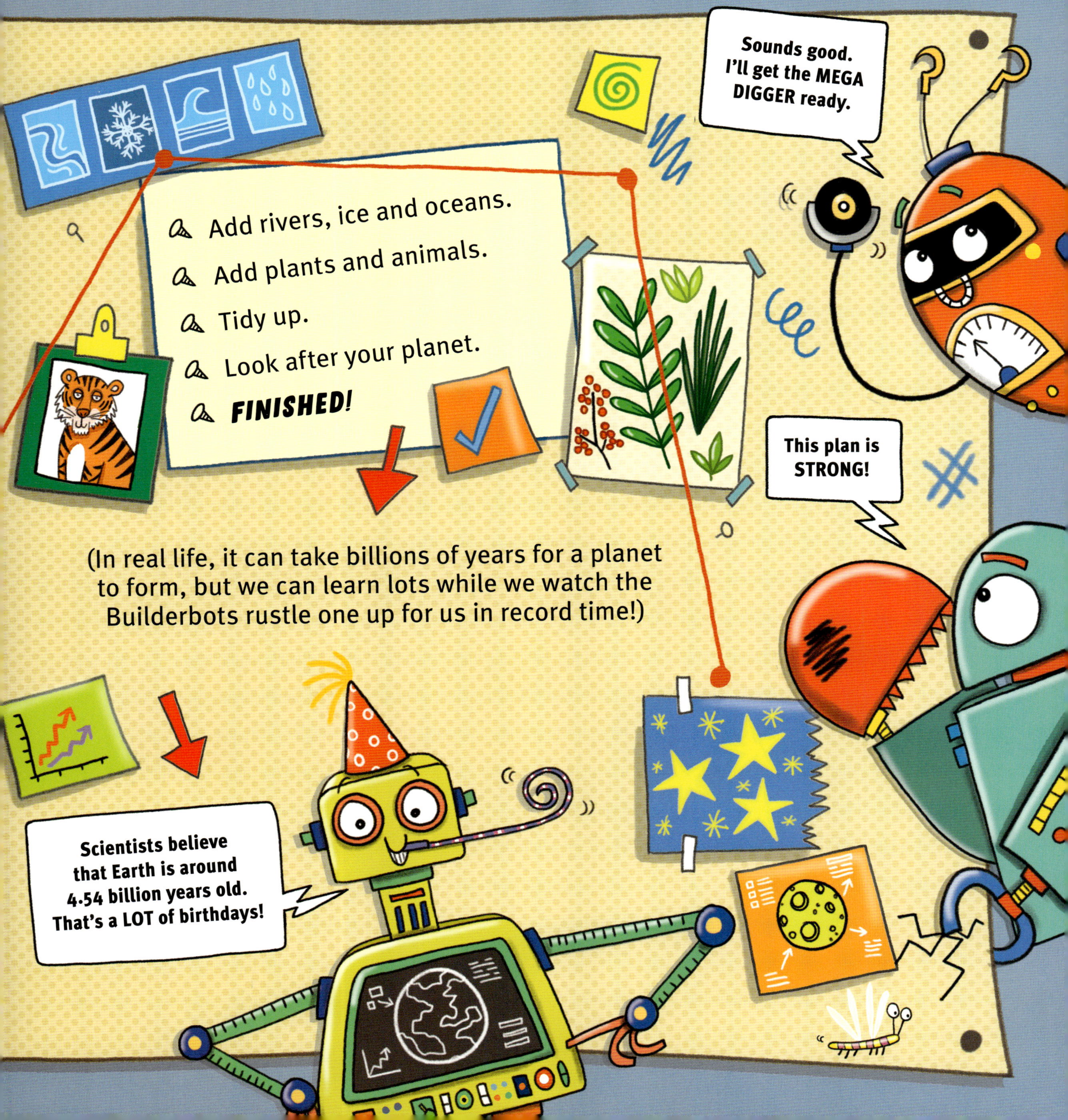

- Add rivers, ice and oceans.
- Add plants and animals.
- Tidy up.
- Look after your planet.
- ***FINISHED!***

Sounds good. I'll get the MEGA DIGGER ready.

This plan is STRONG!

(In real life, it can take billions of years for a planet to form, but we can learn lots while we watch the Builderbots rustle one up for us in record time!)

Scientists believe that Earth is around 4.54 billion years old. That's a LOT of birthdays!

CHOOSE A SPACE ADDRESS

Planets mostly travel round (or "orbit") their nearest star. A star is a huge ball of burning gas that produces lots of heat and light. It allows life to exist on a planet, but only if it's the right distance away.

- **TOO CLOSE** to a star – your planet's life would get **fried.**
- **TOO FAR AWAY** from a star – your planet's life would get **deep-frozen.**
- **JUST RIGHT** – scientists call this distance the **"Goldilocks Zone"**, after the story of *Goldilocks and the Three Bears*. It's where life can **survive.**

In the story, Goldilocks tried porridges that were too HOT and too COLD.

SOLAR WIND WARNING

As it burns, a star sends out a constant stream of particles called "solar wind". Too much solar wind can be deadly dangerous, but a planet is usually safe in the Goldilocks Zone.

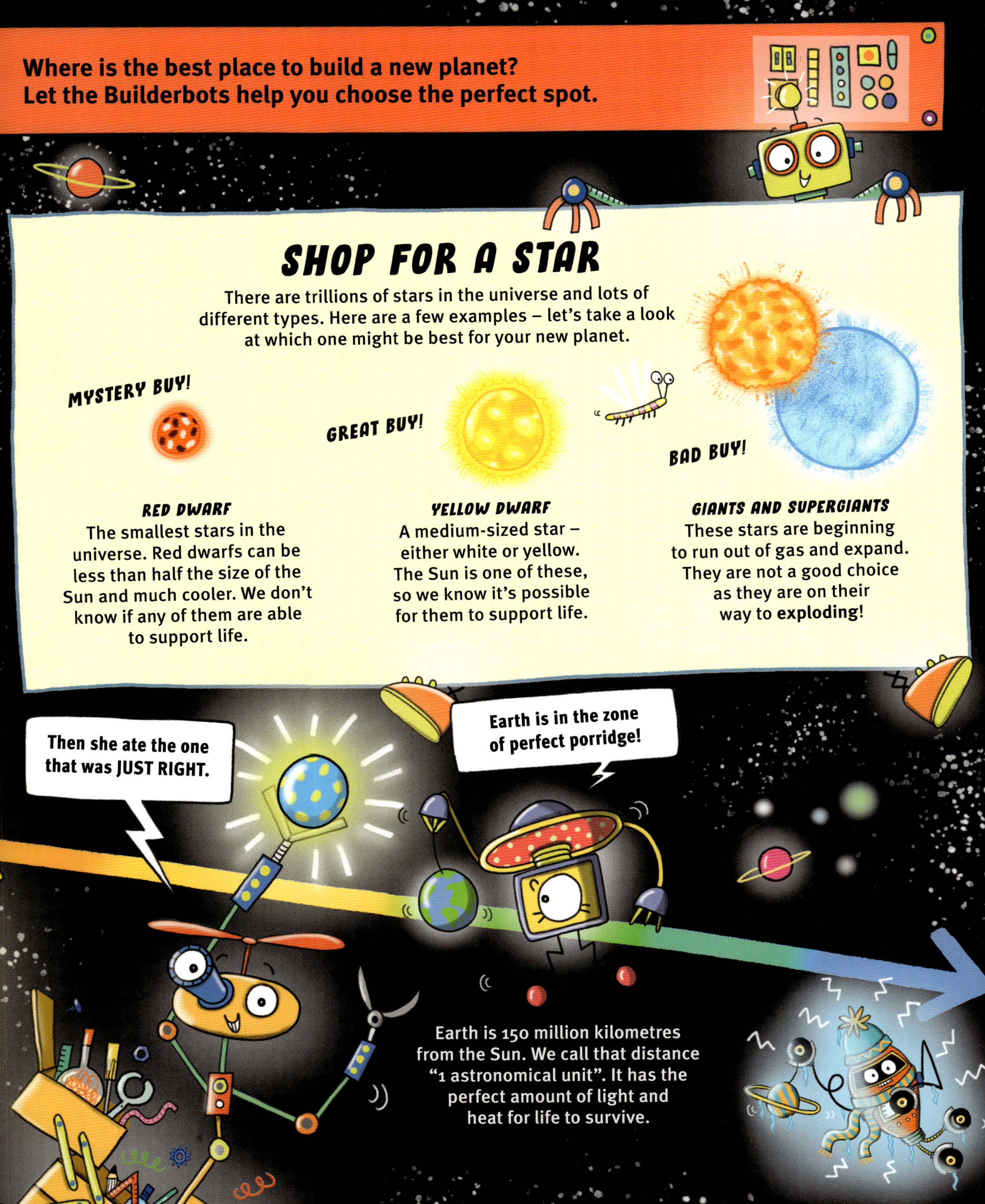

Where is the best place to build a new planet?
Let the Builderbots help you choose the perfect spot.
SHOP FOR A STAR
There are trillions of stars in the universe and lots of different types. Here are a few examples – let's take a look at which one might be best for your new planet.
MYSTERY BUY!
GREAT BUY!
BAD BUY!
RED DWARF
The smallest stars in the universe. Red dwarfs can be less than half the size of the Sun and much cooler. We don't know if any of them are able to support life.
YELLOW DWARF
A medium-sized star – either white or yellow. The Sun is one of these, so we know it's possible for them to support life.
GIANTS AND SUPERGIANTS
These stars are beginning to run out of gas and expand. They are not a good choice as they are on their way to exploding!
Then she ate the one that was JUST RIGHT.
Earth is in the zone of perfect porridge!
Earth is 150 million kilometres from the Sun. We call that distance "1 astronomical unit". It has the perfect amount of light and heat for life to survive.

EXPLORE A NEIGHBOURHOOD

A "solar system" is the name we give to a group of planets that orbit around a star. In the Earth's solar system, there are eight planets – including Earth – zooming round the Sun.

THE SUN – If the Sun was hollow, one million Earths would fit inside it.

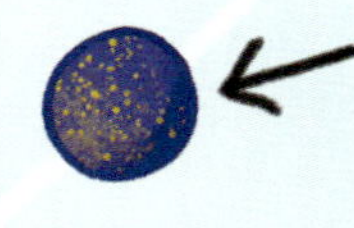

MERCURY – 2.6 times smaller than Earth and way hotter in the daytime. At night, it gets around ten times colder than a deep freezer. (0.4 astronomical units from the Sun.)

VENUS – About the same size as Earth, but here the temperature can get hot enough to melt a tin can. (0.7 astronomical units from the Sun.)

EARTH – One astronomical unit from the Sun. **HELLO, LIFE!**

MARS – About half the size of Earth. Lifeless and mainly dry and dusty. (1.5 astronomical units from the Sun.)

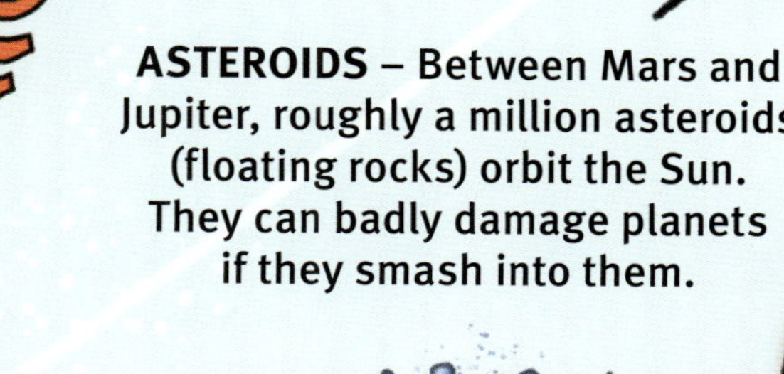

ASTEROIDS – Between Mars and Jupiter, roughly a million asteroids (floating rocks) orbit the Sun. They can badly damage planets if they smash into them.

The star we know the most about is our home star, the Sun. So let's take a look at its solar system before we start building our own.

JUPITER – Eleven times larger than Earth and wrapped in super-cold poisonous gases. (About 5.2 astronomical units from the Sun.)

URANUS – Four times larger than Earth and unbelievably freezing. (Nearly 20 astronomical units from the Sun.)

SATURN – Even colder than Jupiter and just over nine times larger than Earth. (9.5 astronomical units from the Sun.)

NEPTUNE – The coldest planet in the solar system. *Brrrrrrr!* It's nearly four times larger than Earth. (Over 30 astronomical units from the Sun.)

DWARF PLANETS – There are at least five mini planets, called "dwarf planets", in our solar system – and there could be more! The most well-known dwarf planet is Pluto, which is far, far out in the freezing darkness and most likely lifeless.

FIND A PLANET RECIPE

GAS PLANETS

Saturn and Jupiter are mostly made of swirling gases. We call them "gas giants". Underneath the gas clouds, there might be a thick, lumpy soup of chemicals round a core made of rock and metal.

ICY PLANETS

Uranus and Neptune are gas giants, too, but they're also nicknamed "ice giants" because they contain lots of ice, as well.

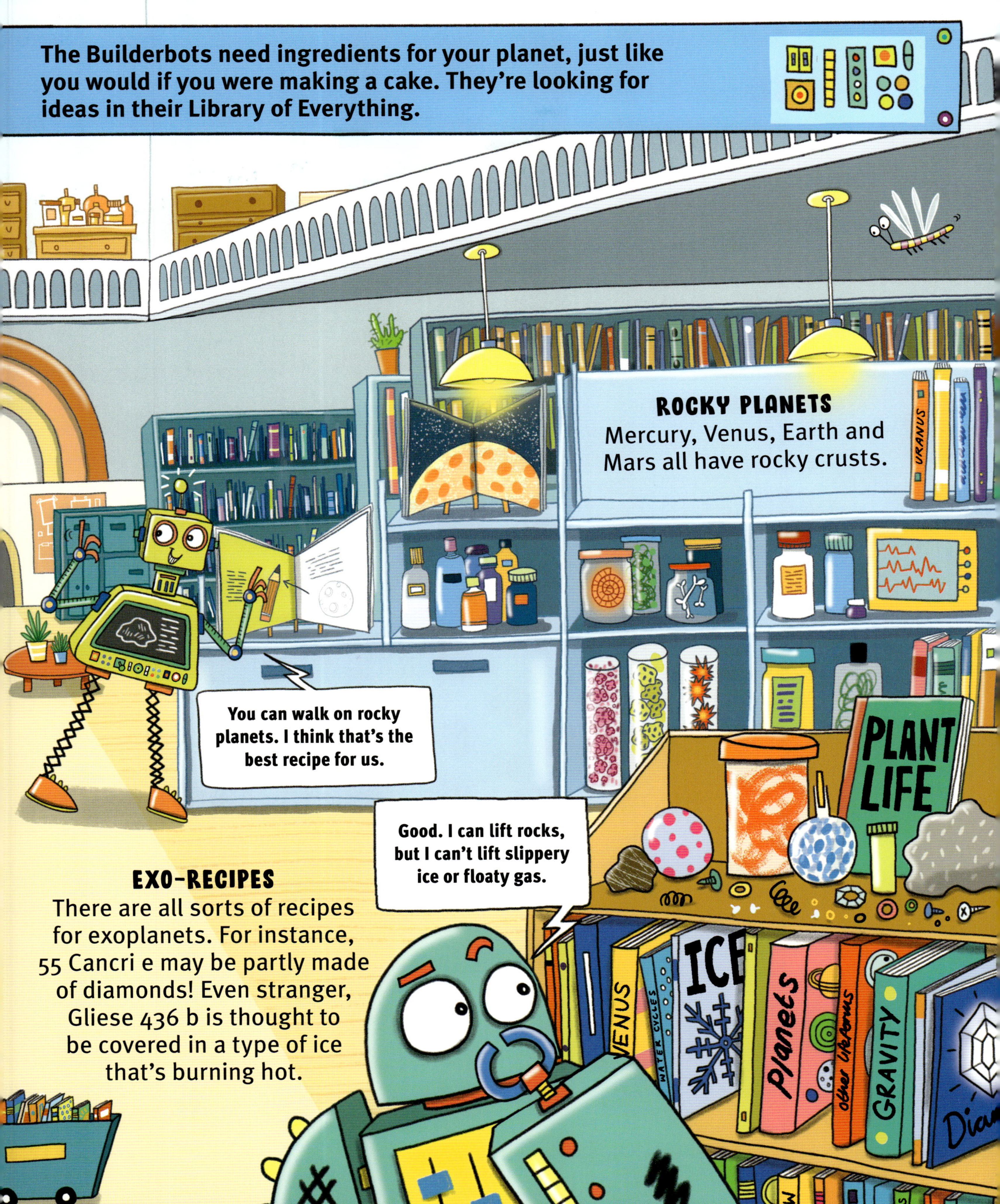
The Builderbots need ingredients for your planet, just like you would if you were making a cake. They're looking for ideas in their Library of Everything.
ROCKY PLANETS
Mercury, Venus, Earth and Mars all have rocky crusts.
URANUS
You can walk on rocky planets. I think that's the best recipe for us.
PLANT LIFE
Good. I can lift rocks, but I can't lift slippery ice or floaty gas.
EXO-RECIPES
There are all sorts of recipes for exoplanets. For instance, 55 Cancri e may be partly made of diamonds! Even stranger, Gliese 436 b is thought to be covered in a type of ice that's burning hot.
VENUS
WATER CYCLES
ICE
Planets
other lifeforms
GRAVITY

THE ROCK STORE
The shelves are stacked with hundreds of different types of rocks. These rocks are mostly made in one of three ways:
IGNEOUS
1. HEATED AND COOLED
When hot molten rock bubbles up from underground, it cools and hardens into different kinds of **igneous** (*ig*-nee-us) rock. Igneous rocks are often found around volcanoes.
Pumice
Scoria
Granite
Obsidian
Ironstone
Chert
Diabase
Pegmatite
Basalt
Peridotite
Gabbro

Skipper has sent the team to the Rock Store to get supplies for our mega planet-building project.

SEDIMENTARY

2. SQUASHED AND SQUEEZED

Sedimentary (sed-ee-*men*-tary) rocks are made from broken pieces of other rocks that get buried, then squeezed and squashed for millions of years. Sedimentary rock crumbles into grains of sand and makes beaches.

METAMORPHIC

3. HEATED AND SQUEEZED

Sometimes, igneous and sedimentary rocks get pushed way down towards a planet's centre. There, they are changed into **metamorphic** (met-uh-*mor*-fic) rocks by heat and squeezing. Earth's highest mountains are made from metamorphic rock.

It is thought that some exoplanets are made of unusual rocks not seen on Earth. Some space rocks might even be soft like a pillow, or perhaps very easily melted, like a bar of chocolate on a warm day.

START BUILDING

The crust of a rocky planet is like a giant version of an eggshell. The Builderbots have got some smashing plans for yours . . .

Now the Builderbots can get started on the new planet. They're using the Earth recipe they found in the library.

4. Inner core
In the middle of the Earth, there's a giant, solid ball of mixed-up metals – mostly iron. It's as hot as the surface of the Sun.

THE BIGGEST JIGSAW EVER

The tectonic plates are all different shapes and sizes. Toolbox T has drawn a map of the biggest ones.

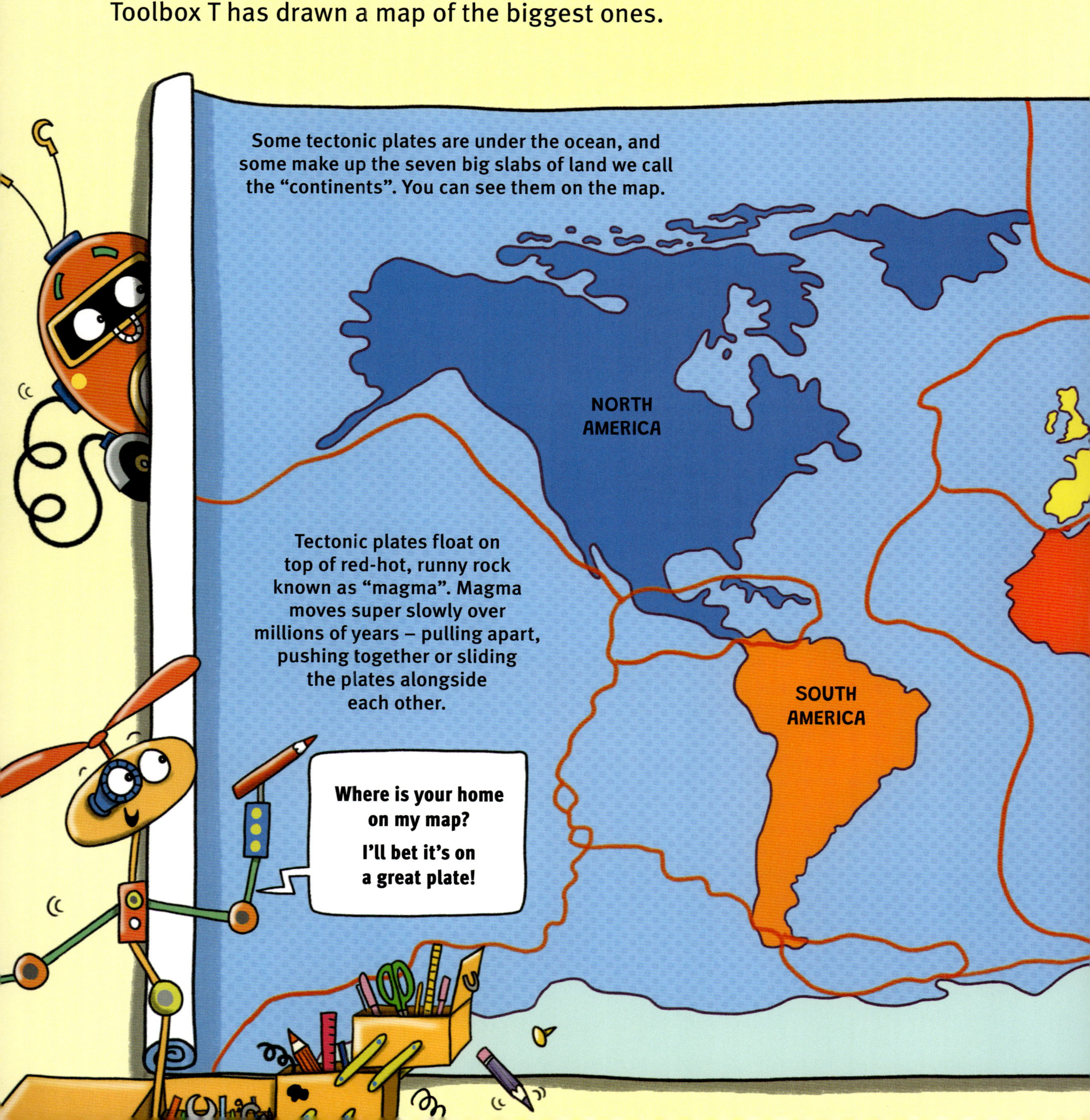

The Earth's crust is broken up into sections called "tectonic plates". These plates are like giant jigsaw pieces.
Earth is super special. It's the only planet we know of that has floating plates.
The movement of the plates creates all sorts of incredible things, such as mountains and volcanoes.
EUROPE
ASIA
FRICA
OCEANIA
ANTARCTICA
Talking of plates, I think it's snack time!

BOOM! SHAKE!

If you've got magma moving beneath the planet's surface, it will sometimes burst out of cracks between the plates.

Now your new planet has moving tectonic plates, like those on Earth, there are going to be volcanoes and earthquakes.

A volcano that has erupted recently is called **"active"**. **Dormant** volcanoes are volcanoes that haven't erupted in a while, but they may still erupt again one day. **Extinct** volcanoes aren't expected to ever erupt again.

Gases and ash also billow out.

ASH

GASES

Earth's tallest volcano is **MAUNA KEA** in Hawaii. It's taller than the world's highest mountain, but most of it is hidden under the sea.

STROMBOLI is a volcano off the coast of Italy. It has small eruptions every 20–30 minutes.

Waaah! I'm rattling all over!

PLATES = QUAKES

Earthquakes happen when two plates slide against each other and make the Earth's crust shudder. Shockwaves called **"tremors"** ripple through the ground, making everything shake.

CRUNCH! PUSH!

FOLD MOUNTAINS

When two plates shove against each other, land folds upward and downward along the join. We call this a "fold mountain range".

Earth's highest mountain range, the Himalayas, is made up of fold mountains. They are still rising, too, as one giant plate pushes underneath another.

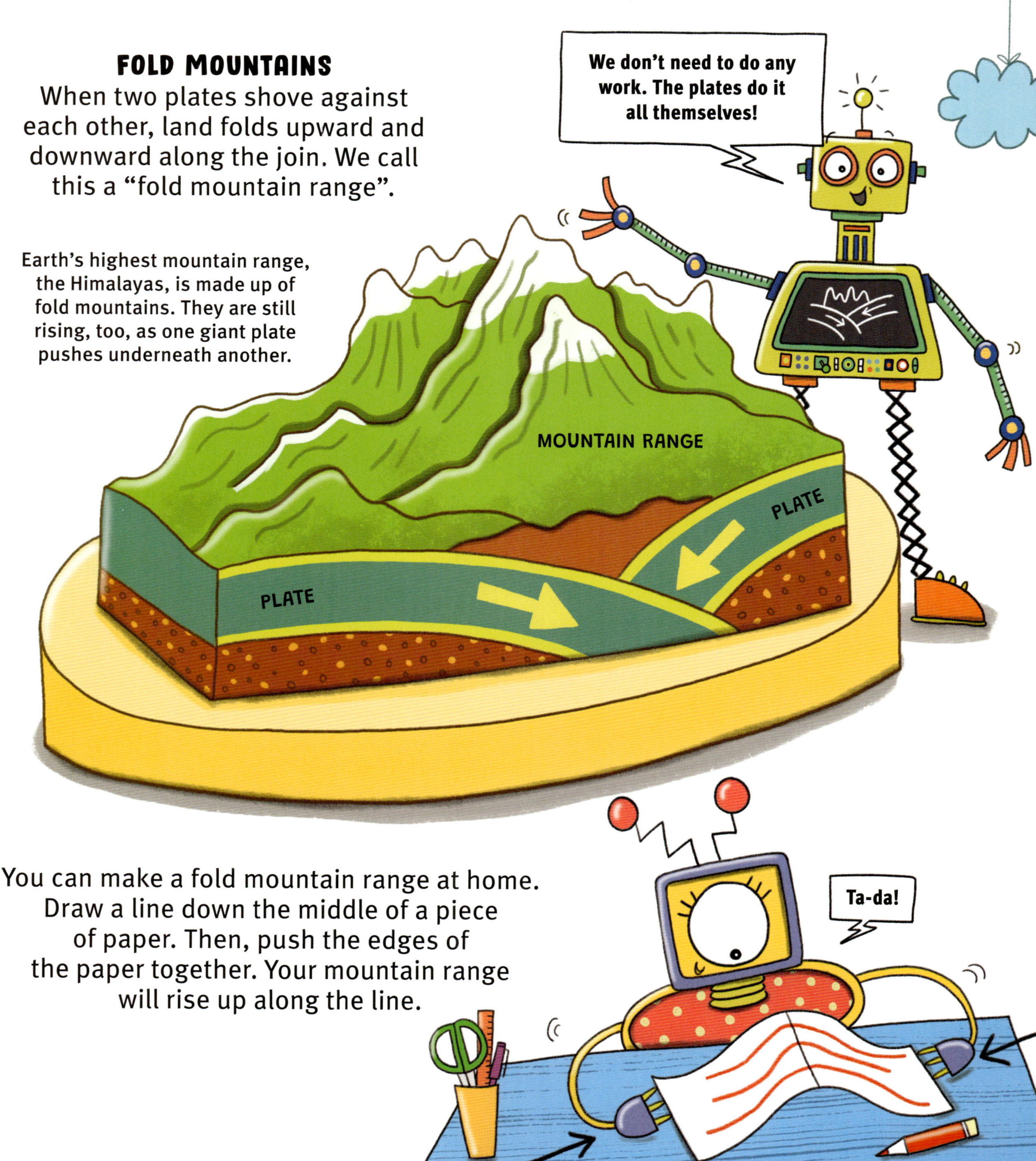

You can make a fold mountain range at home. Draw a line down the middle of a piece of paper. Then, push the edges of the paper together. Your mountain range will rise up along the line.

When the Earth's tectonic plates pull and push, they create mountains very slowly. There are different kinds.

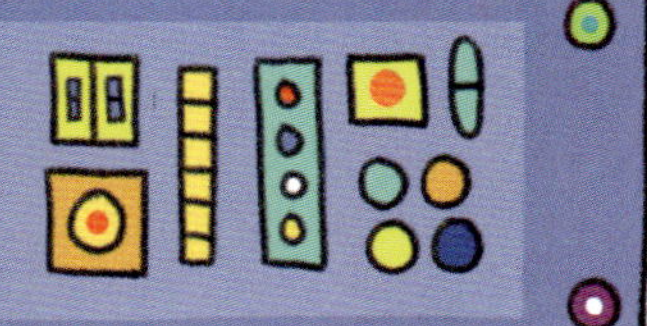

BLOCK MOUNTAINS

Block mountains are made when two plates pull apart from each other. A giant piece of land breaks off in the middle and rises up.

In the United States of America, California's Sierra Nevada mountain range is made up of block mountains.

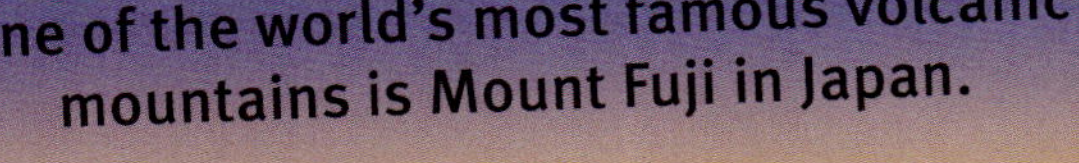

One of the world's most famous volcanic mountains is Mount Fuji in Japan.

VOLCANIC MOUNTAINS

Some mountains build up and up after volcanic eruptions.

SPACE MOUNTAINS

Yes, there are mountains in space! Mars has a huge volcanic mountain called Olympus Mons. It's about three times as high as Mount Everest. And Skadi Mons, a mountain on Venus, is coated in poisonous metallic snow!

PLAN SOME MOVES!

DAY AND NIGHT

All the planets that we know about spin on an "axis" (an imaginary line running through the centre of a planet). Earth spinning is the reason we have daytime and night-time.

The Earth takes 23 hours and 56 minutes to spin round once on its axis.

The Sun's light only shines on one side of Earth at a time. When it's daytime on the shiny side, it's night-time on the dark side.

As the Earth spins, the sides gradually change round. Daytime becomes night-time and night-time becomes daytime.

Once your planet is ready, the Builderbots will set it in orbit and then spin it round!

THE TILT

Earth travels through space slightly tilted on its axis. That's the reason our planet has seasons.

It takes 365.25 days for the Earth to travel round the Sun – that's twelve months, or one year.

For six months per year, one half of the planet is tilted towards the Sun, while the other half is tilted away. Then, for the next six months, they swap.

The half of the planet that is closest to the Sun gets warmer weather. The other half gets colder weather.

DOING IT DIFFERENTLY

Other planets might spin much faster or slower than Earth.

A year on K2-137 b lasts 4.3 Earth hours, and one year on exoplanet CVSO 30c lasts for 27,000 Earth years!

I like having years that aren't too long. I don't want to wait ages for my birthday!

WHAT TO BREATHE

WHICH GASES?

An atmosphere is made of a mix of different gases. Earth's atmosphere is mainly nitrogen and oxygen – and it's the only mix that humans can safely breathe. All the other planets we know about have atmospheres made of deadly gases.

WHICH COLOUR?

The gases in Earth's atmosphere don't have any colour, but they interact with sunlight to make the sky look blue. Mars often has pinky-red skies because its atmosphere is full of dust. Venus's atmosphere of poisonous gases looks orangey-yellow.

Would you like to keep your planet safe and cosy? Then you'll need an "atmosphere". It can help in lots of ways, just as Earth's atmosphere helps Earth.

HOW MUCH PRESSURE?

Earth's atmosphere presses on everyone, but it usually feels comfortable for human bodies. That's not true of all atmospheres out in space, though. The atmospheric pressure on Venus is around 95 times heavier than on Earth, and it would crush a human flat in an instant. Yikes!

Out in space, humans must wear a pressurized spacesuit. A spacesuit comfortably squeezes the body, copying the pressure on Earth.

Gases are pumped round the spacesuit. It's like wearing a human-shaped balloon.

When a meteor hits Earth, it's called a "meteorite".

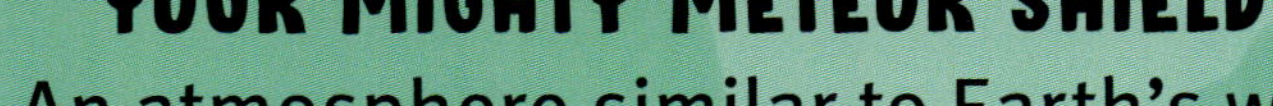

YOUR MIGHTY METEOR SHIELD

An atmosphere similar to Earth's will protect your planet by keeping it warm and shielding it from dangerous space radiation. It will also protect you from meteors – lumps of rock that hurtle through space.

When meteors zoom towards Earth, they heat up while speeding through all the gas molecules in the atmosphere. Most burn up before they get to the ground.

WELCOME TO THE WEATHER

WINDY WORLD

Wind happens when gas molecules move around in the atmosphere. On Earth, air molecules rise and start whizzing about when they get warm. As the warm molecules move up, colder air molecules rush in below to replace them.

The Sun heats up the Earth's air molecules. It warms the Earth's land and oceans, and that heat radiates up and warms the air.

Wind is lots of busy, bustling gas molecules!

Sometimes fearsome storms rage. These are called "hurricanes". They happen when there's lots of water vapour in the air and lots of air molecules whizzing around, too.

Jupiter is home to a megastorm called the "Great Red Spot" that has been raging for more than 300 years!

Once an atmosphere is filled with gases, they will swirl around and sometimes create strong winds. If your planet is like Earth, it will rain, too.

WATERY WORLD

Earth is lucky enough to have lots of water. It falls from the sky as rain, filling up rivers, lakes and oceans. Plants and animals need it to survive.

When the Sun heats up the water on Earth, it evaporates, which means it turns into water vapour floating in the air.

The vapour gradually joins together to make droplets. The droplets gather into clouds.

Eventually, the clouds get so heavy that the water falls back to the Earth as rain or snow.

Earth's water goes round and round – making water vapour, then rain or snow, then rivers and seas.

CARVE WITH WATER

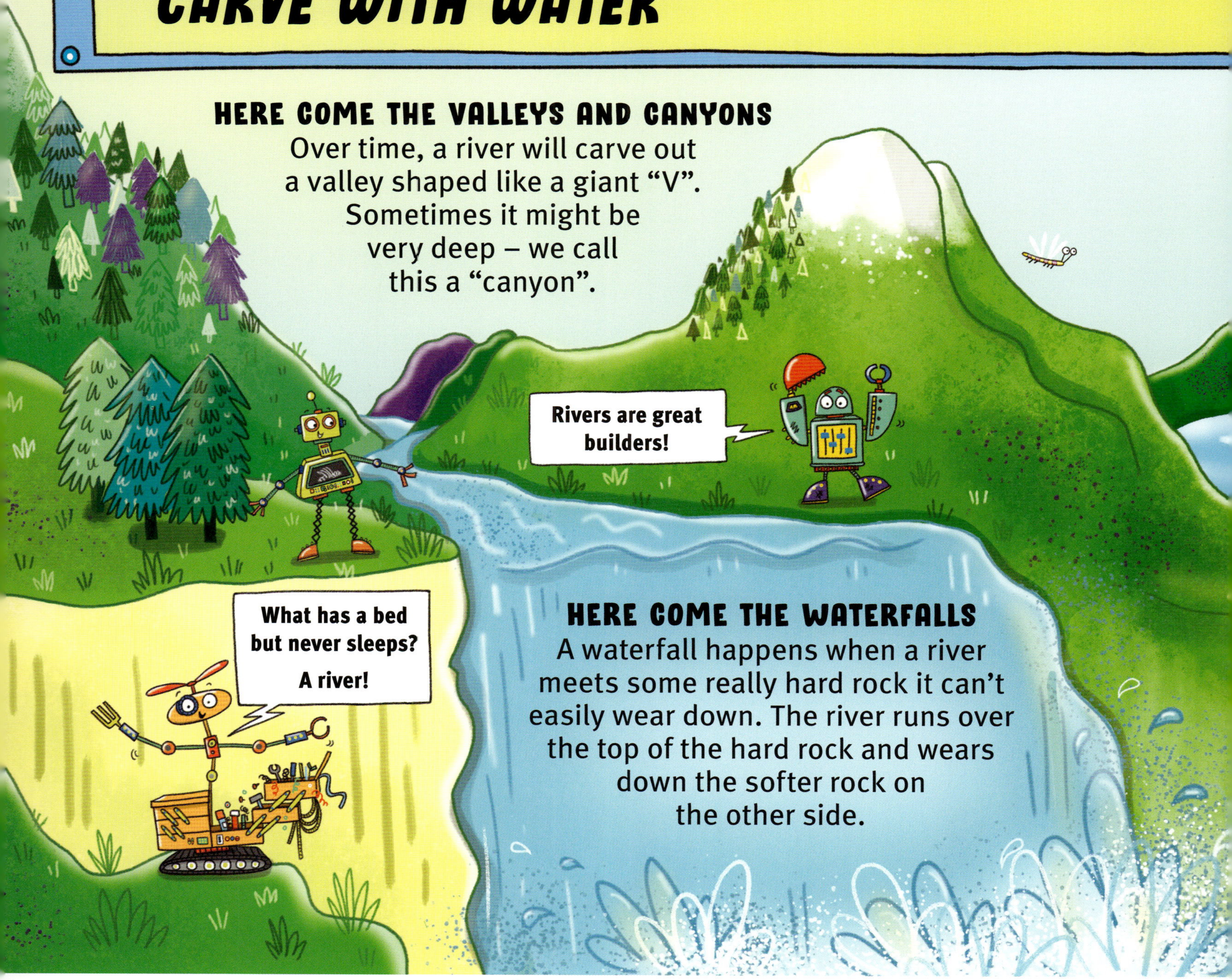

HERE COME THE VALLEYS AND CANYONS

Over time, a river will carve out a valley shaped like a giant "V". Sometimes it might be very deep – we call this a "canyon".

Rivers are great builders!

What has a bed but never sleeps? A river!

HERE COME THE WATERFALLS

A waterfall happens when a river meets some really hard rock it can't easily wear down. The river runs over the top of the hard rock and wears down the softer rock on the other side.

Earth's deepest open canyon is the Yarlung Tsangpo Grand Canyon in Tibet. In some places, the canyon walls are more than 5,300 metres high.

Earth's biggest waterfall is Africa's Victoria Falls, also called Mosi-oa-Tunya ("The Smoke that Thunders"). At peak times, its water flow would fill 3.75 million bathtubs a minute!

Flowing rivers change the shape of the land, and so does ice.

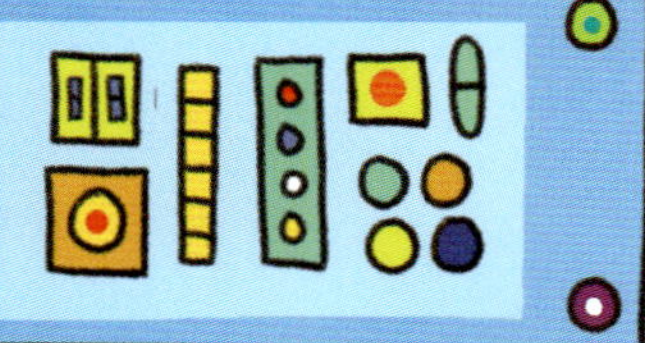

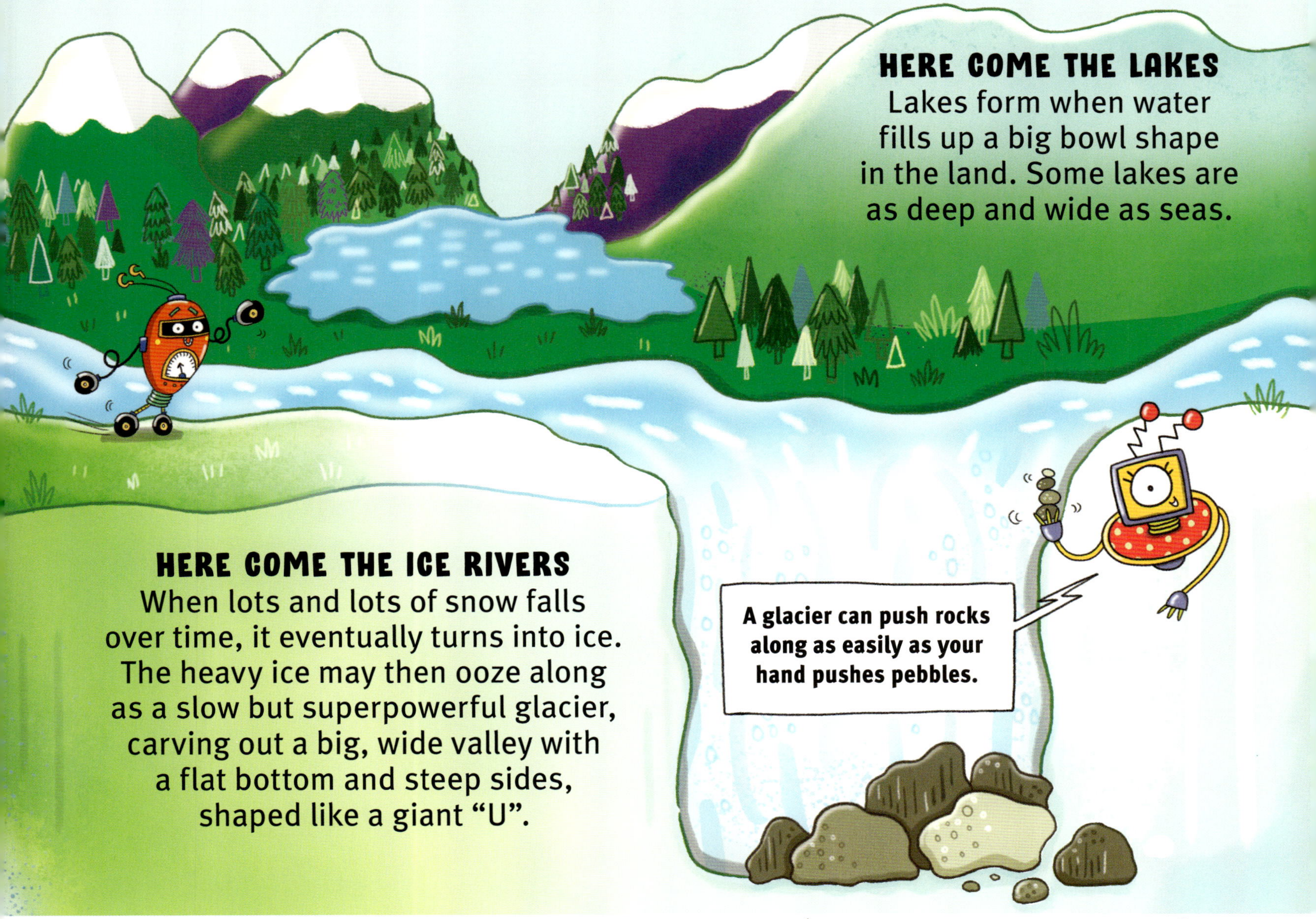

HERE COME THE LAKES

Lakes form when water fills up a big bowl shape in the land. Some lakes are as deep and wide as seas.

HERE COME THE ICE RIVERS

When lots and lots of snow falls over time, it eventually turns into ice. The heavy ice may then ooze along as a slow but superpowerful glacier, carving out a big, wide valley with a flat bottom and steep sides, shaped like a giant "U".

A glacier can push rocks along as easily as your hand pushes pebbles.

Earth's biggest lake is the Caspian Sea (so it's not really a sea). It stretches for nearly 1,200 kilometres through Central Asia.

The Matterhorn is a famous craggy mountain in Switzerland. Its pointy shape was carved by glaciers, which shows just how powerful they are.

MAKE SOME OCEANS

CHOOSE FROM THE SALTY-SEA SHOPPING LIST . . .

A WARM OCEAN FOR SWIMMING

The Indian Ocean is Earth's warmest ocean. Sometimes, at the surface, it is the temperature of a lukewarm bath.

A COLD, ICY OCEAN FOR ICE SHEETS

The Arctic Ocean and the Southern Ocean are both so cold that they sometimes freeze over.

A DEEP OCEAN FOR STEEP-SIDED TRENCHES

Trenches are underwater canyons. The Mariana Trench in the Pacific Ocean is Earth's deepest, plunging for more than 11 kilometres.

A SHALLOW OCEAN FOR CORAL REEFS

Coral usually grows in shallow seas. The Great Barrier Reef is the biggest coral reef on Earth. It stretches for thousands of kilometres off the north-east coast of Australia.

Earth has different sorts of oceans. What do you think they should be like on your planet?

DON'T FORGET THE SALT!

Rain washes chemicals from the soil and rocks into Earth's oceans, making the water salty.

OCEAN SHAPES

When the sea meets the land and wears the rock down, it can create different shapes. Look out for these ones . . .

GROW SOME PLANTS

START WITH SOIL

Most plants need soil because it contains the nutrients (useful chemicals) and water they need to stay healthy. Soil is made of grains of rock and tiny pieces of dead animals and plants. It soaks up rainwater, too.

The other rocky planets in our solar system don't have soil. They only have rock dust, called "regolith". Scientists have grown plants in regolith from the Moon, but only by mixing it with extra nutrients and water.

WHY IS SOIL SO SPECIAL?

The top layer of soil is where plants grow. It takes hundreds of years to form, so it's very precious stuff. Around 95 per cent of the food that humans eat depends on soil. It's vital for life on Earth!

Adding plants and trees will make your planet extra special. The Builderbots will do the gardening for you, so let's grow!

Plants are good for you and the planet. Win-win!

GIVE YOUR PLANTS LIGHT

Unlike animals, green plants can make their food from scratch. It's their superpower! To do that, they need light.

Green plants contain chlorophyll (*klo*-row-fill), which absorbs energy from sunlight. The leaves also absorb a gas from the air called "carbon dioxide". The roots take up water from the soil . . . And now the plant has what it needs to get food-making!

SUNLIGHT

CARBON DIOXIDE

SUGAR

OXYGEN

WATER

Plants use the Sun's energy to change carbon dioxide and water into sugar, which they then use to help them grow. In doing this, they also create oxygen, which humans breathe. The food-making is called "photosynthesizing" (foe-toe-*sin*-thuh-size-ing).

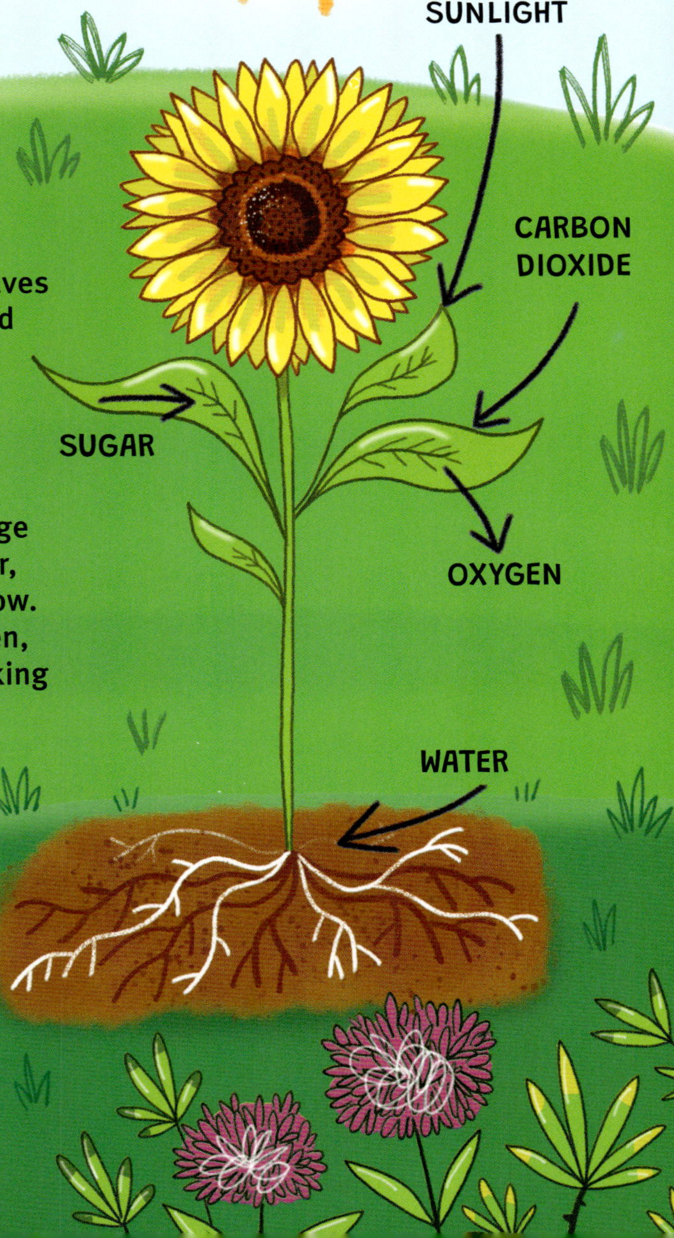

Plants are amazing! They help make Earth healthy for humans.

PLANT ALL SORTS

Parasitic plants fasten on to other plants and steal their food! The giant padma – a plant with the world's biggest flower – steals its food from nearby vines in Indonesian rainforests.

Trees grow in all sorts of shapes and sizes, from redwoods as high as 35-storey skyscrapers to tiny dwarf willows the size of your little finger.

Cacti are famous for their spikes. On some cacti, they can grow as long as an adult human's middle finger.

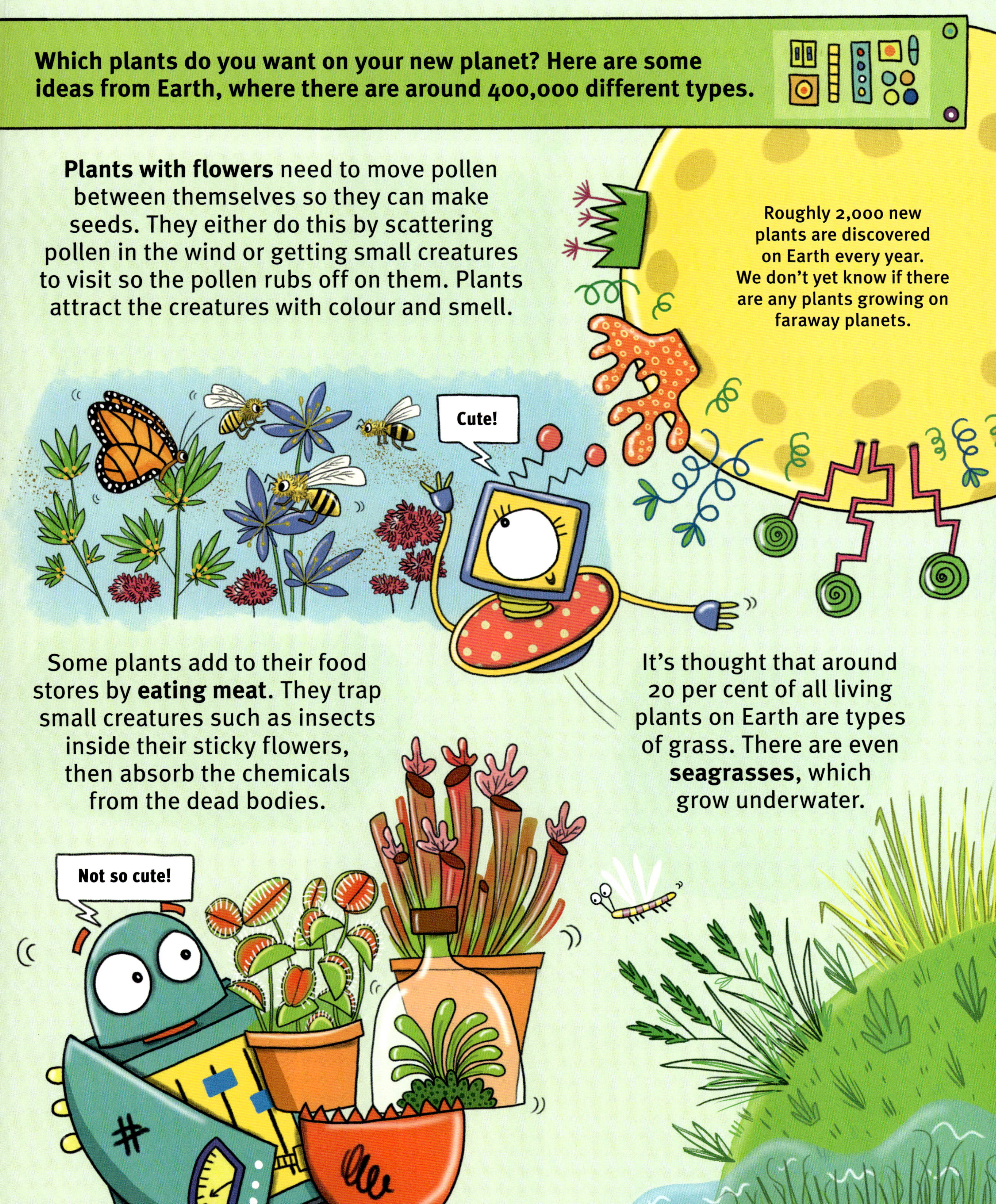

Which plants do you want on your new planet? Here are some ideas from Earth, where there are around 400,000 different types.

Plants with flowers need to move pollen between themselves so they can make seeds. They either do this by scattering pollen in the wind or getting small creatures to visit so the pollen rubs off on them. Plants attract the creatures with colour and smell.

Roughly 2,000 new plants are discovered on Earth every year. We don't yet know if there are any plants growing on faraway planets.

Some plants add to their food stores by **eating meat**. They trap small creatures such as insects inside their sticky flowers, then absorb the chemicals from the dead bodies.

It's thought that around 20 per cent of all living plants on Earth are types of grass. There are even **seagrasses**, which grow underwater.

ANIMALS ARRIVE

Birds are animals with feathers, born from hard-shelled eggs.

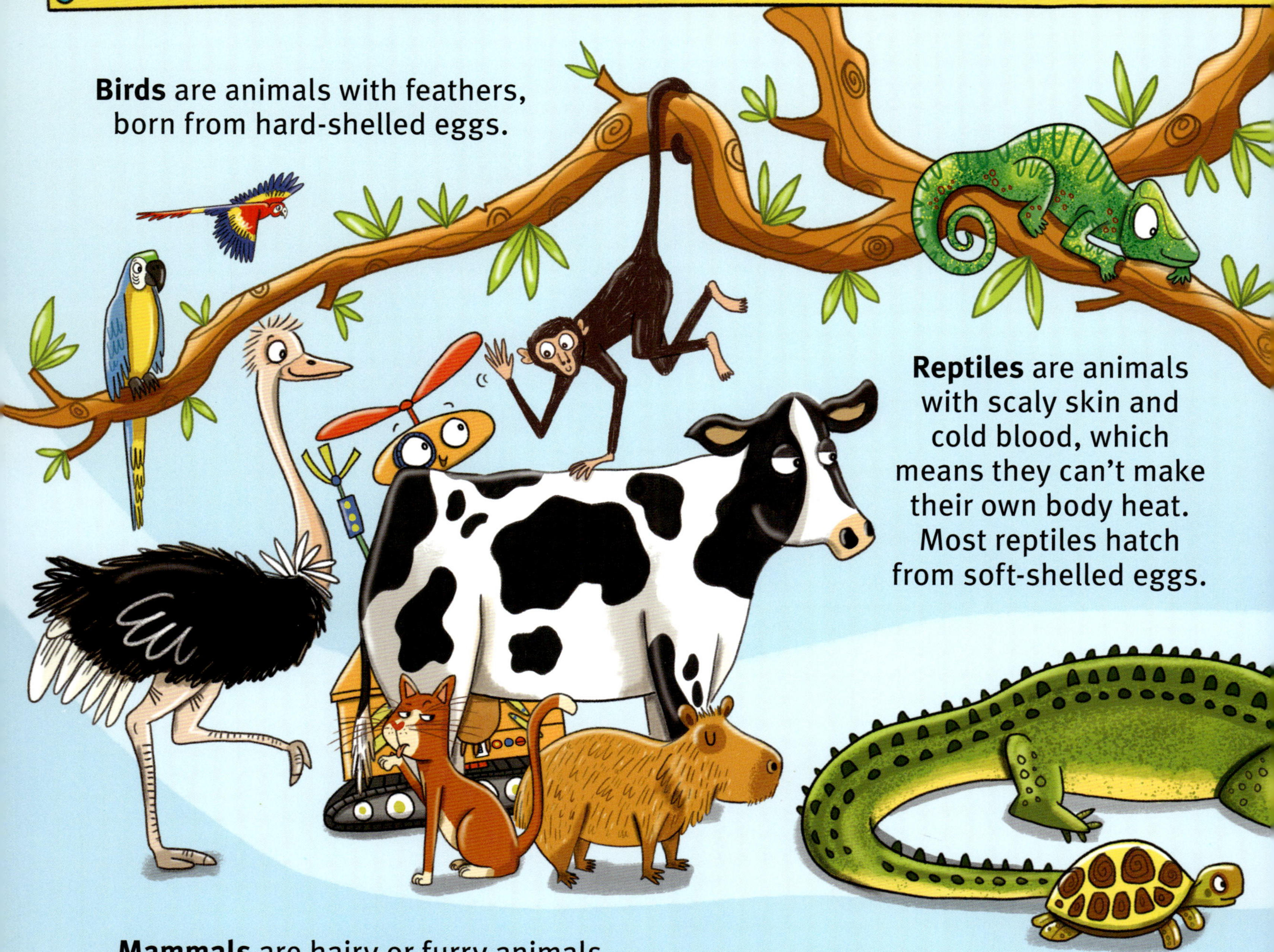

Reptiles are animals with scaly skin and cold blood, which means they can't make their own body heat. Most reptiles hatch from soft-shelled eggs.

Mammals are hairy or furry animals that drink their mother's milk when they are born. This group includes humans.

Tiny organisms called **"microbes"** live just about everywhere on Earth. Roughly a billion microbes live in one teaspoon of healthy soil. They are good at surviving in tough conditions, so perhaps they even live on other planets already!

With plants and soil, your planet can become home to animals. Here are some major animal groups on Earth.

Fish are animals with fins. They live in water and breathe through gills.

Amphibians are damp-skinned animals born in water but also able to live on land.

Insects are animals with six legs and an exoskeleton (a hard outer covering) instead of bones.

FOOD FOR THE ANIMALS

Around 33 per cent of Earth's animals only eat plants. They are called **"herbivores"**. Earth's biggest land animal, the African elephant, is a herbivore.

Around 63 per cent of Earth's animals eat other animals. They're called **"carnivores"**. They include many fearsome hunters.

We need to think about how your planet will feed all your cool animals! Let's take some tips from what happens on Planet Earth.

Roughly 4 per cent of Earth's animals are able to eat both plants and animals. They're called **"omnivores"**. Humans are omnivores.

BIG EATERS

The biggest blue whales eat 10 to 20 tons or more of shrimp-like krill each day. That's roughly the equivalent of 70,000 to 80,000 burgers in buns!

Adult male grizzly bears eat more than 40 kilograms of food each day in summer, often including around 40,000 moths and up to 100,000 berries.

YOUR PLANET IS READY!

The International Astronomical Union decides on names for all space objects and planet features, such as mountains and craters. When planets are first spotted, they are given the name of their nearest galaxy, plus lots of numbers and letters that show when and how they were spotted. Later, they might get a name that's easier to remember.

Most of the planets in Earth's solar system were named after ancient Greek or Roman gods centuries ago. More recently, newly discovered exoplanets have been named after gods and goddesses from many different cultures.

Is there a person you like who could inspire your planet's name? They could be a famous person or someone you know. They could be a made-up character from a story or a TV show, perhaps.

You can decide!

Wow! Great job, Builderbots! Now you just need to give your new world a name. Here are some ideas to help you decide.

Gandalf and Bilbo are both characters from *The Lord of the Rings* and the names of mountains on Saturn!

Hooray!

In the 1980s, an astronomer named an asteroid after his cat, Mr Spock.

HOORAY!

I declare this planet OPEN!

Hooray!

The planet Draugr was named after a zombie horse from a Viking myth.

LOOK AFTER YOUR PLANET!

1. KEEP YOUR PLANET CLEAN
Litter causes pollution, which is dangerous to animals and humans.

2. DON'T WASTE WHAT YOU HAVE
Recycle and reuse as much as you can.

3. CARE FOR YOUR CREATURES
Otherwise they will die out, and your planet won't be anywhere near as beautiful or interesting.